SHE DID BECAUSE SHE COULD

FITNESS JOURNAL AND PLANNER

INSPIRA

JOURNALS, PLANNERS &
NOTEBOOKS

THIS BOOK BELONGS TO:

_____

FOOD LOG

DAY

DATE

WEEK #

GOAL FOR TODAY

BREAKFAST   TIME:

FOOD/BEVERAGE	Calories	Carbs	Fat	Protein
SUBTOTAL				

LUNCH   TIME:

FOOD/BEVERAGE	Calories	Carbs	Fat	Protein
SUBTOTAL				

SNACKS

TIME:

FOOD/BEVERAGE	Calories	Carbs	Fat	Protein
SUBTOTAL				

DINNER

TIME:

FOOD/BEVERAGE	Calories	Carbs	Fat	Protein
SUBTOTAL				

TOTAL				

WATER INTAKE

DAILY FOOD GOALS

TARGET	ACTUAL	
		calories
		protein
		carbs
		fat

FITNESS LOG

TO DO

- ☐ ....
- ☐ ....
- ☐ ....
- ☐ ....
- ☐ ....

GOAL FOR TODAY

TIME OF DAY:

CARDIO / OTHER	Heart Rate	Duration	Speed	Level	Intensity	Other	Calories used
SUBTOTAL							

NOTES

TIME OF DAY:

WEIGHTS	Heart Rate	Duration	Speed	Level	Intensity	Other	Calories used
SUBTOTAL							

TOTAL							

VITAMINS / SUPPLEMENTS	DOSAGE	QUANTITY

JOURNAL

FOOD LOG

DAY	DATE	WEEK #

- ☐ ....
- ☐ ....
- ☐ ....
- ☐ ....
- ☐ ....

GOAL FOR TODAY

BREAKFAST   TIME:

FOOD/BEVERAGE	Calories	Carbs	Fat	Protein
SUBTOTAL				

LUNCH   TIME:

FOOD/BEVERAGE	Calories	Carbs	Fat	Protein
SUBTOTAL				

SNACKS

TIME:

FOOD/BEVERAGE	Calories	Carbs	Fat	Protein
SUBTOTAL				

DINNER

TIME:

FOOD/BEVERAGE	Calories	Carbs	Fat	Protein
SUBTOTAL				

TOTAL				

WATER INTAKE

DAILY FOOD GOALS

TARGET	ACTUAL	
		calories
		protein
		carbs
		fat

FITNESS LOG

TO DO

- ☐ ....
- ☐ ....
- ☐ ....
- ☐ ....
- ☐ ....

GOAL FOR TODAY

TIME OF DAY:

CARDIO / OTHER	Heart Rate	Duration	Speed	Level	Intensity	Other	Calories used
SUBTOTAL							

NOTES

TIME OF DAY:

WEIGHTS	Heart Rate	Duration	Speed	Level	Intensity	Other	Calories used
SUBTOTAL							

TOTAL							

VITAMINS / SUPPLEMENTS	DOSAGE	QUANTITY

JOURNAL

FOOD LOG

DAY	DATE	WEEK #

TO DO

- ☐ ....
- ☐ ....
- ☐ ....
- ☐ ....
- ☐ ....

GOAL FOR TODAY

BREAKFAST   TIME:

FOOD/BEVERAGE	Calories	Carbs	Fat	Protein
SUBTOTAL				

LUNCH   TIME:

FOOD/BEVERAGE	Calories	Carbs	Fat	Protein
SUBTOTAL				

SNACKS

TIME:

FOOD/BEVERAGE	Calories	Carbs	Fat	Protein
SUBTOTAL				

DINNER

TIME:

FOOD/BEVERAGE	Calories	Carbs	Fat	Protein
SUBTOTAL				

TOTAL				

WATER INTAKE

DAILY FOOD GOALS

TARGET	ACTUAL	
		calories
		protein
		carbs
		fat

FITNESS LOG

☐ ....

☐ ....

☐ ....

☐ ....

☐ ....

GOAL FOR TODAY

TIME OF DAY:

CARDIO / OTHER	Heart Rate	Duration	Speed	Level	Intensity	Other	Calories used
SUBTOTAL							

NOTES

TIME OF DAY:

WEIGHTS	Heart Rate	Duration	Speed	Level	Intensity	Other	Calories used
SUBTOTAL							

TOTAL							

VITAMINS / SUPPLEMENTS	DOSAGE	QUANTITY

JOURNAL

FOOD LOG

DAY

DATE

WEEK #

TO DO

- ☐ ....
- ☐ ....
- ☐ ....
- ☐ ....
- ☐ ....

GOAL FOR TODAY

BREAKFAST	TIME:			
FOOD/BEVERAGE	Calories	Carbs	Fat	Protein
SUBTOTAL				

LUNCH	TIME:			
FOOD/BEVERAGE	Calories	Carbs	Fat	Protein
SUBTOTAL				

SNACKS   TIME:

FOOD/BEVERAGE	Calories	Carbs	Fat	Protein
SUBTOTAL				

DINNER   TIME:

FOOD/BEVERAGE	Calories	Carbs	Fat	Protein
SUBTOTAL				

TOTAL				

WATER INTAKE

DAILY FOOD GOALS

TARGET	ACTUAL	
		calories
		protein
		carbs
		fat

FITNESS LOG

TO DO

- ☐ ....
- ☐ ....
- ☐ ....
- ☐ ....
- ☐ ....

GOAL FOR TODAY

TIME OF DAY:

CARDIO / OTHER	Heart Rate	Duration	Speed	Level	Intensity	Other	Calories used
SUBTOTAL							

NOTES

TIME OF DAY:

WEIGHTS	Heart Rate	Duration	Speed	Level	Intensity	Other	Calories used
SUBTOTAL							

TOTAL							

VITAMINS / SUPPLEMENTS	DOSAGE	QUANTITY

JOURNAL

FOOD LOG

DAY	DATE	WEEK #

TO DO

- ☐ ....
- ☐ ....
- ☐ ....
- ☐ ....
- ☐ ....

GOAL FOR TODAY

BREAKFAST		TIME:		
FOOD/BEVERAGE	Calories	Carbs	Fat	Protein
SUBTOTAL				

LUNCH		TIME:		
FOOD/BEVERAGE	Calories	Carbs	Fat	Protein
SUBTOTAL				

SNACKS

TIME:

FOOD/BEVERAGE	Calories	Carbs	Fat	Protein
SUBTOTAL				

DINNER

TIME:

FOOD/BEVERAGE	Calories	Carbs	Fat	Protein
SUBTOTAL				

TOTAL				

WATER INTAKE

DAILY FOOD GOALS

TARGET	ACTUAL	
		calories
		protein
		carbs
		fat

FITNESS LOG

TO DO

- ☐ ....
- ☐ ....
- ☐ ....
- ☐ ....
- ☐ ....

GOAL FOR TODAY

TIME OF DAY:

CARDIO / OTHER	Heart Rate	Duration	Speed	Level	Intensity	Other	Calories used
SUBTOTAL							

NOTES

TIME OF DAY:

WEIGHTS	Heart Rate	Duration	Speed	Level	Intensity	Other	Calories used
SUBTOTAL							

TOTAL							

VITAMINS / SUPPLEMENTS	DOSAGE	QUANTITY

JOURNAL

PROGRESS

STATS	Weight	BMI	BMR	Heart Rate	Cholesterol	Blood Sugar	Other

MEASUREMENT

Neck	Shoulder	Chest	Waist

Hip	Thigh	Calf	Arm

NOTES

....
....
....
....
....
....
....
....
....
....
....
....

FOOD LOG

DAY

DATE

WEEK #

TO DO
- ☐ ....
- ☐ ....
- ☐ ....
- ☐ ....
- ☐ ....

GOAL FOR TODAY

BREAKFAST — TIME:

FOOD/BEVERAGE	Calories	Carbs	Fat	Protein
SUBTOTAL				

LUNCH — TIME:

FOOD/BEVERAGE	Calories	Carbs	Fat	Protein
SUBTOTAL				

SNACKS   TIME:

FOOD/BEVERAGE	Calories	Carbs	Fat	Protein
SUBTOTAL				

DINNER   TIME:

FOOD/BEVERAGE	Calories	Carbs	Fat	Protein
SUBTOTAL				

TOTAL				

WATER INTAKE

DAILY FOOD GOALS

TARGET	ACTUAL	
		calories
		protein
		carbs
		fat

FITNESS LOG

TO DO

- [ ] ....
- [ ] ....
- [ ] ....
- [ ] ....
- [ ] ....

GOAL FOR TODAY

TIME OF DAY:

CARDIO / OTHER	Heart Rate	Duration	Speed	Level	Intensity	Other	Calories used
SUBTOTAL							

NOTES

TIME OF DAY:

WEIGHTS	Heart Rate	Duration	Speed	Level	Intensity	Other	Calories used
SUBTOTAL							

TOTAL							

VITAMINS / SUPPLEMENTS	DOSAGE	QUANTITY

JOURNAL

FOOD LOG

DAY

DATE

WEEK #

TO DO

- ☐ ....
- ☐ ....
- ☐ ....
- ☐ ....
- ☐ ....

GOAL FOR TODAY

BREAKFAST
TIME:

FOOD/BEVERAGE	Calories	Carbs	Fat	Protein
SUBTOTAL				

LUNCH
TIME:

FOOD/BEVERAGE	Calories	Carbs	Fat	Protein
SUBTOTAL				

SNACKS

TIME:

FOOD/BEVERAGE	Calories	Carbs	Fat	Protein
SUBTOTAL				

DINNER

TIME:

FOOD/BEVERAGE	Calories	Carbs	Fat	Protein
SUBTOTAL				

TOTAL				

WATER INTAKE

DAILY FOOD GOALS

TARGET	ACTUAL	
		calories
		protein
		carbs
		fat

FITNESS LOG

TO DO

- ☐ ....
- ☐ ....
- ☐ ....
- ☐ ....
- ☐ ....

GOAL FOR TODAY

TIME OF DAY:

CARDIO / OTHER	Heart Rate	Duration	Speed	Level	Intensity	Other	Calories used
SUBTOTAL							

NOTES

TIME OF DAY:

WEIGHTS	Heart Rate	Duration	Speed	Level	Intensity	Other	Calories used
SUBTOTAL							

TOTAL							

VITAMINS / SUPPLEMENTS	DOSAGE	QUANTITY

JOURNAL

FOOD LOG

DAY

DATE

WEEK

TO DO

- ☐ ....
- ☐ ....
- ☐ ....
- ☐ ....
- ☐ ....

GOAL FOR TODAY

BREAKFAST   TIME:

FOOD/BEVERAGE	Calories	Carbs	Fat	Protein
SUBTOTAL				

LUNCH   TIME:

FOOD/BEVERAGE	Calories	Carbs	Fat	Protein
SUBTOTAL				

SNACKS

TIME:

FOOD/BEVERAGE	Calories	Carbs	Fat	Protein
SUBTOTAL				

DINNER

TIME:

FOOD/BEVERAGE	Calories	Carbs	Fat	Protein
SUBTOTAL				

TOTAL				

WATER INTAKE

DAILY FOOD GOALS

TARGET	ACTUAL	
		calories
		protein
		carbs
		fat

FITNESS LOG

TO DO

- ☐ ....
- ☐ ....
- ☐ ....
- ☐ ....
- ☐ ....

GOAL FOR TODAY

TIME OF DAY:

CARDIO / OTHER	Heart Rate	Duration	Speed	Level	Intensity	Other	Calories used
SUBTOTAL							

NOTES

TIME OF DAY:

WEIGHTS	Heart Rate	Duration	Speed	Level	Intensity	Other	Calories used
SUBTOTAL							

TOTAL							

VITAMINS / SUPPLEMENTS	DOSAGE	QUANTITY

JOURNAL

FOOD LOG

DAY	DATE	WEEK #

TO DO

- ☐ ....
- ☐ ....
- ☐ ....
- ☐ ....
- ☐ ....

GOAL FOR TODAY

BREAKFAST

TIME:

FOOD/BEVERAGE	Calories	Carbs	Fat	Protein
SUBTOTAL				

LUNCH

TIME:

FOOD/BEVERAGE	Calories	Carbs	Fat	Protein
SUBTOTAL				

SNACKS

TIME:

FOOD/BEVERAGE	Calories	Carbs	Fat	Protein
SUBTOTAL				

DINNER

TIME:

FOOD/BEVERAGE	Calories	Carbs	Fat	Protein
SUBTOTAL				

TOTAL				

WATER INTAKE

DAILY FOOD GOALS

TARGET	ACTUAL	
		calories
		protein
		carbs
		fat

FITNESS LOG

TO DO

- ☐ ....
- ☐ ....
- ☐ ....
- ☐ ....
- ☐ ....

GOAL FOR TODAY

TIME OF DAY:

CARDIO / OTHER	Heart Rate	Duration	Speed	Level	Intensity	Other	Calories used
SUBTOTAL							

NOTES

TIME OF DAY:

WEIGHTS	Heart Rate	Duration	Speed	Level	Intensity	Other	Calories used
SUBTOTAL							

TOTAL							

VITAMINS / SUPPLEMENTS	DOSAGE	QUANTITY

JOURNAL

FOOD LOG

DAY	DATE	WEEK #

TO DO

- ☐ ....
- ☐ ....
- ☐ ....
- ☐ ....
- ☐ ....

GOAL FOR TODAY

BREAKFAST TIME:

FOOD/BEVERAGE	Calories	Carbs	Fat	Protein
SUBTOTAL				

LUNCH TIME:

FOOD/BEVERAGE	Calories	Carbs	Fat	Protein
SUBTOTAL				

SNACKS

TIME:

FOOD/BEVERAGE	Calories	Carbs	Fat	Protein
SUBTOTAL				

DINNER

TIME:

FOOD/BEVERAGE	Calories	Carbs	Fat	Protein
SUBTOTAL				

TOTAL				

WATER INTAKE

DAILY FOOD GOALS

TARGET	ACTUAL	
		calories
		protein
		carbs
		fat

FITNESS LOG

TO DO

- ☐ ....
- ☐ ....
- ☐ ....
- ☐ ....
- ☐ ....

GOAL FOR TODAY

TIME OF DAY:

CARDIO / OTHER	Heart Rate	Duration	Speed	Level	Intensity	Other	Calories used
SUBTOTAL							

NOTES

TIME OF DAY:

WEIGHTS	Heart Rate	Duration	Speed	Level	Intensity	Other	Calories used
SUBTOTAL							

TOTAL							

VITAMINS / SUPPLEMENTS	DOSAGE	QUANTITY

JOURNAL

FOOD LOG

DAY	DATE	WEEK #

TO DO

- ☐ ....
- ☐ ....
- ☐ ....
- ☐ ....
- ☐ ....

GOAL FOR TODAY

BREAKFAST   TIME:

FOOD/BEVERAGE	Calories	Carbs	Fat	Protein
SUBTOTAL				

LUNCH   TIME:

FOOD/BEVERAGE	Calories	Carbs	Fat	Protein
SUBTOTAL				

SNACKS   TIME:

FOOD/BEVERAGE	Calories	Carbs	Fat	Protein
SUBTOTAL				

DINNER   TIME:

FOOD/BEVERAGE	Calories	Carbs	Fat	Protein
SUBTOTAL				

TOTAL				

WATER INTAKE

DAILY FOOD GOALS

TARGET	ACTUAL	
		calories
		protein
		carbs
		fat

FITNESS LOG

TO DO

- ☐ ....
- ☐ ....
- ☐ ....
- ☐ ....
- ☐ ....

GOAL FOR TODAY

TIME OF DAY:

CARDIO / OTHER	Heart Rate	Duration	Speed	Level	Intensity	Other	Calories used
SUBTOTAL							

NOTES

TIME OF DAY:

WEIGHTS	Heart Rate	Duration	Speed	Level	Intensity	Other	Calories used
SUBTOTAL							

TOTAL							

VITAMINS / SUPPLEMENTS	DOSAGE	QUANTITY

JOURNAL

THE PAIN
YOU FEEL TODAY
WILL BE THE
STRENGTH
YOU FEEL TOMORROW

PROGRESS

STATS	Weight	BMI	BMR	Heart Rate	Cholesterol	Blood Sugar	Other

MEASUREMENT

Neck	Shoulder	Chest	Waist

Hip	Thigh	Calf	Arm

NOTES

....

....

....

....

....

....

....

....

....

....

....

....

FOOD LOG

DAY	DATE	WEEK #

TO DO

- ☐ ....
- ☐ ....
- ☐ ....
- ☐ ....
- ☐ ....

GOAL FOR TODAY

BREAKFAST   TIME:

FOOD/BEVERAGE	Calories	Carbs	Fat	Protein
SUBTOTAL				

LUNCH   TIME:

FOOD/BEVERAGE	Calories	Carbs	Fat	Protein
SUBTOTAL				

SNACKS

TIME:

FOOD/BEVERAGE	Calories	Carbs	Fat	Protein
SUBTOTAL				

DINNER

TIME:

FOOD/BEVERAGE	Calories	Carbs	Fat	Protein
SUBTOTAL				

TOTAL				

WATER INTAKE

DAILY FOOD GOALS

TARGET	ACTUAL	
		calories
		protein
		carbs
		fat

FITNESS LOG

TO DO

- ☐ ....
- ☐ ....
- ☐ ....
- ☐ ....
- ☐ ....

GOAL FOR TODAY

TIME OF DAY:

CARDIO / OTHER	Heart Rate	Duration	Speed	Level	Intensity	Other	Calories used
SUBTOTAL							

NOTES

TIME OF DAY:

WEIGHTS	Heart Rate	Duration	Speed	Level	Intensity	Other	Calories used
SUBTOTAL							

TOTAL							

VITAMINS / SUPPLEMENTS	DOSAGE	QUANTITY

JOURNAL

FOOD LOG

DAY	DATE	WEEK #

TO DO

- ☐ ....
- ☐ ....
- ☐ ....
- ☐ ....
- ☐ ....

GOAL FOR TODAY

BREAKFAST   TIME:

FOOD/BEVERAGE	Calories	Carbs	Fat	Protein
SUBTOTAL				

LUNCH   TIME:

FOOD/BEVERAGE	Calories	Carbs	Fat	Protein
SUBTOTAL				

SNACKS   TIME:

FOOD/BEVERAGE	Calories	Carbs	Fat	Protein
SUBTOTAL				

DINNER   TIME:

FOOD/BEVERAGE	Calories	Carbs	Fat	Protein
SUBTOTAL				

TOTAL				

WATER INTAKE

DAILY FOOD GOALS

TARGET	ACTUAL	
		calories
		protein
		carbs
		fat

FITNESS LOG

TO DO

- ☐ ....
- ☐ ....
- ☐ ....
- ☐ ....
- ☐ ....

GOAL FOR TODAY

TIME OF DAY:

CARDIO / OTHER	Heart Rate	Duration	Speed	Level	Intensity	Other	Calories used
SUBTOTAL							

NOTES

TIME OF DAY:

WEIGHTS	Heart Rate	Duration	Speed	Level	Intensity	Other	Calories used
SUBTOTAL							

TOTAL							

VITAMINS / SUPPLEMENTS	DOSAGE	QUANTITY

JOURNAL

FOOD LOG

DAY	DATE	WEEK #

TO DO

- ☐ ....
- ☐ ....
- ☐ ....
- ☐ ....
- ☐ ....

GOAL FOR TODAY

BREAKFAST		TIME:		
FOOD/BEVERAGE	Calories	Carbs	Fat	Protein
SUBTOTAL				

LUNCH		TIME:		
FOOD/BEVERAGE	Calories	Carbs	Fat	Protein
SUBTOTAL				

SNACKS

TIME:

FOOD/BEVERAGE	Calories	Carbs	Fat	Protein
SUBTOTAL				

DINNER

TIME:

FOOD/BEVERAGE	Calories	Carbs	Fat	Protein
SUBTOTAL				

TOTAL				

WATER INTAKE

DAILY FOOD GOALS

TARGET	ACTUAL	
		calories
		protein
		carbs
		fat

FITNESS LOG

TO DO

☐ ....
☐ ....
☐ ....
☐ ....
☐ ....

GOAL FOR TODAY

TIME OF DAY:

CARDIO / OTHER	Heart Rate	Duration	Speed	Level	Intensity	Other	Calories used
SUBTOTAL							

NOTES

TIME OF DAY:

WEIGHTS	Heart Rate	Duration	Speed	Level	Intensity	Other	Calories used
SUBTOTAL							

TOTAL							

VITAMINS / SUPPLEMENTS	DOSAGE	QUANTITY

JOURNAL

FOOD LOG

DAY	DATE	WEEK #

TO DO

- ☐ ....
- ☐ ....
- ☐ ....
- ☐ ....
- ☐ ....

GOAL FOR TODAY

BREAKFAST — TIME:

FOOD/BEVERAGE	Calories	Carbs	Fat	Protein
SUBTOTAL				

LUNCH — TIME:

FOOD/BEVERAGE	Calories	Carbs	Fat	Protein
SUBTOTAL				

SNACKS

TIME:

FOOD/BEVERAGE	Calories	Carbs	Fat	Protein
SUBTOTAL				

DINNER

TIME:

FOOD/BEVERAGE	Calories	Carbs	Fat	Protein
SUBTOTAL				

TOTAL				

WATER INTAKE

DAILY FOOD GOALS

TARGET	ACTUAL	
		calories
		protein
		carbs
		fat

FITNESS LOG

TO DO

- ☐ ....
- ☐ ....
- ☐ ....
- ☐ ....
- ☐ ....

GOAL FOR TODAY

TIME OF DAY:

CARDIO / OTHER	Heart Rate	Duration	Speed	Level	Intensity	Other	Calories used
SUBTOTAL							

NOTES

TIME OF DAY:

WEIGHTS	Heart Rate	Duration	Speed	Level	Intensity	Other	Calories used
SUBTOTAL							

TOTAL							

VITAMINS / SUPPLEMENTS	DOSAGE	QUANTITY

JOURNAL

FOOD LOG

DAY	DATE	WEEK #

TO DO

- ☐ ....
- ☐ ....
- ☐ ....
- ☐ ....
- ☐ ....

GOAL FOR TODAY

BREAKFAST   TIME:

FOOD/BEVERAGE	Calories	Carbs	Fat	Protein
SUBTOTAL				

LUNCH   TIME:

FOOD/BEVERAGE	Calories	Carbs	Fat	Protein
SUBTOTAL				

SNACKS   TIME:

FOOD/BEVERAGE	Calories	Carbs	Fat	Protein
SUBTOTAL				

DINNER   TIME:

FOOD/BEVERAGE	Calories	Carbs	Fat	Protein
SUBTOTAL				

TOTAL				

WATER INTAKE

DAILY FOOD GOALS

TARGET	ACTUAL	
		calories
		protein
		carbs
		fat

FITNESS LOG

TO DO

- ☐ ....
- ☐ ....
- ☐ ....
- ☐ ....
- ☐ ....

GOAL FOR TODAY

TIME OF DAY:

CARDIO / OTHER	Heart Rate	Duration	Speed	Level	Intensity	Other	Calories used
SUBTOTAL							

NOTES

TIME OF DAY:

WEIGHTS	Heart Rate	Duration	Speed	Level	Intensity	Other	Calories used
SUBTOTAL							

TOTAL							

VITAMINS / SUPPLEMENTS	DOSAGE	QUANTITY

JOURNAL

PROGRESS

	Weight	BMI	BMR	Heart Rate	Cholesterol	Blood Sugar	Other
STATS							

MEASUREMENT

Neck	Shoulder	Chest	Waist

Hip	Thigh	Calf	Arm

NOTES

....

....

....

....

....

....

....

....

....

....

....

....

....

FOOD LOG

DAY

DATE

WEEK #

TO DO

- ☐ ....
- ☐ ....
- ☐ ....
- ☐ ....
- ☐ ....

GOAL FOR TODAY

BREAKFAST   TIME:

FOOD/BEVERAGE	Calories	Carbs	Fat	Protein
SUBTOTAL				

LUNCH   TIME:

FOOD/BEVERAGE	Calories	Carbs	Fat	Protein
SUBTOTAL				

SNACKS

TIME:

FOOD/BEVERAGE	Calories	Carbs	Fat	Protein
SUBTOTAL				

DINNER

TIME:

FOOD/BEVERAGE	Calories	Carbs	Fat	Protein
SUBTOTAL				

TOTAL				

WATER INTAKE

DAILY FOOD GOALS

TARGET	ACTUAL	
		calories
		protein
		carbs
		fat

FITNESS LOG

TO DO

- [ ] ....
- [ ] ....
- [ ] ....
- [ ] ....
- [ ] ....

GOAL FOR TODAY

TIME OF DAY:

CARDIO / OTHER	Heart Rate	Duration	Speed	Level	Intensity	Other	Calories used
SUBTOTAL							

NOTES

TIME OF DAY:

WEIGHTS	Heart Rate	Duration	Speed	Level	Intensity	Other	Calories used
SUBTOTAL							

TOTAL							

VITAMINS / SUPPLEMENTS	DOSAGE	QUANTITY

JOURNAL

FOOD LOG

DAY

DATE

WEEK #

TO DO

- ☐ ....
- ☐ ....
- ☐ ....
- ☐ ....
- ☐ ....

GOAL FOR TODAY

BREAKFAST

TIME:

FOOD/BEVERAGE	Calories	Carbs	Fat	Protein
SUBTOTAL				

LUNCH

TIME:

FOOD/BEVERAGE	Calories	Carbs	Fat	Protein
SUBTOTAL				

SNACKS   TIME:

FOOD/BEVERAGE	Calories	Carbs	Fat	Protein
SUBTOTAL				

DINNER   TIME:

FOOD/BEVERAGE	Calories	Carbs	Fat	Protein
SUBTOTAL				

TOTAL				

WATER INTAKE

DAILY FOOD GOALS

TARGET	ACTUAL	
		calories
		protein
		carbs
		fat

FITNESS LOG

TO DO

- ☐ ....
- ☐ ....
- ☐ ....
- ☐ ....
- ☐ ....

GOAL FOR TODAY

TIME OF DAY:

CARDIO / OTHER	Heart Rate	Duration	Speed	Level	Intensity	Other	Calories used
SUBTOTAL							

NOTES

TIME OF DAY:

WEIGHTS	Heart Rate	Duration	Speed	Level	Intensity	Other	Calories used
SUBTOTAL							

TOTAL							

VITAMINS / SUPPLEMENTS	DOSAGE	QUANTITY

JOURNAL

FOOD LOG

DAY	DATE	WEEK #

TO DO

- ☐ ....
- ☐ ....
- ☐ ....
- ☐ ....
- ☐ ....

GOAL FOR TODAY

BREAKFAST   TIME:

FOOD/BEVERAGE	Calories	Carbs	Fat	Protein
SUBTOTAL				

LUNCH   TIME:

FOOD/BEVERAGE	Calories	Carbs	Fat	Protein
SUBTOTAL				

SNACKS	TIME:			
FOOD/BEVERAGE	Calories	Carbs	Fat	Protein
SUBTOTAL				

DINNER	TIME:			
FOOD/BEVERAGE	Calories	Carbs	Fat	Protein
SUBTOTAL				

TOTAL				

WATER INTAKE

DAILY FOOD GOALS

TARGET	ACTUAL	
		calories
		protein
		carbs
		fat

FITNESS LOG

TO DO

- [ ] ....
- [ ] ....
- [ ] ....
- [ ] ....
- [ ] ....

GOAL FOR TODAY

TIME OF DAY:

CARDIO / OTHER	Heart Rate	Duration	Speed	Level	Intensity	Other	Calories used
SUBTOTAL							

NOTES

TIME OF DAY:

WEIGHTS	Heart Rate	Duration	Speed	Level	Intensity	Other	Calories used
SUBTOTAL							

TOTAL							

VITAMINS / SUPPLEMENTS	DOSAGE	QUANTITY

JOURNAL

FOOD LOG

DAY

DATE

WEEK #

TO DO

- ☐ ....
- ☐ ....
- ☐ ....
- ☐ ....
- ☐ ....

GOAL FOR TODAY

BREAKFAST

TIME:

FOOD/BEVERAGE	Calories	Carbs	Fat	Protein
SUBTOTAL				

LUNCH

TIME:

FOOD/BEVERAGE	Calories	Carbs	Fat	Protein
SUBTOTAL				

SNACKS

TIME:

FOOD/BEVERAGE	Calories	Carbs	Fat	Protein
SUBTOTAL				

DINNER

TIME:

FOOD/BEVERAGE	Calories	Carbs	Fat	Protein
SUBTOTAL				

TOTAL				

WATER
INTAKE

DAILY FOOD GOALS

TARGET	ACTUAL	
		calories
		protein
		carbs
		fat

FITNESS LOG

TO DO

- ☐ ....
- ☐ ....
- ☐ ....
- ☐ ....
- ☐ ....

GOAL FOR TODAY

TIME OF DAY:

CARDIO / OTHER	Heart Rate	Duration	Speed	Level	Intensity	Other	Calories used
SUBTOTAL							

NOTES

TIME OF DAY:

WEIGHTS	Heart Rate	Duration	Speed	Level	Intensity	Other	Calories used
SUBTOTAL							

TOTAL							

VITAMINS / SUPPLEMENTS	DOSAGE	QUANTITY

JOURNAL

FOOD LOG

DAY

DATE

WEEK #

TO DO

- [ ] ....
- [ ] ....
- [ ] ....
- [ ] ....
- [ ] ....

GOAL FOR TODAY

BREAKFAST

TIME:

FOOD/BEVERAGE	Calories	Carbs	Fat	Protein
SUBTOTAL				

LUNCH

TIME:

FOOD/BEVERAGE	Calories	Carbs	Fat	Protein
SUBTOTAL				

SNACKS

TIME:

FOOD/BEVERAGE	Calories	Carbs	Fat	Protein
SUBTOTAL				

DINNER

TIME:

FOOD/BEVERAGE	Calories	Carbs	Fat	Protein
SUBTOTAL				

TOTAL				

WATER INTAKE

DAILY FOOD GOALS

TARGET	ACTUAL	
		calories
		protein
		carbs
		fat

FITNESS LOG

TO DO

- ☐ ....
- ☐ ....
- ☐ ....
- ☐ ....
- ☐ ....

GOAL FOR TODAY

TIME OF DAY:

CARDIO / OTHER	Heart Rate	Duration	Speed	Level	Intensity	Other	Calories used
SUBTOTAL							

NOTES

TIME OF DAY:

WEIGHTS	Heart Rate	Duration	Speed	Level	Intensity	Other	Calories used
SUBTOTAL							

TOTAL							

VITAMINS / SUPPLEMENTS	DOSAGE	QUANTITY

JOURNAL

FOOD LOG

DAY

DATE

WEEK #

TO DO

- ☐ ....
- ☐ ....
- ☐ ....
- ☐ ....
- ☐ ....

GOAL FOR TODAY

BREAKFAST   TIME:

FOOD/BEVERAGE	Calories	Carbs	Fat	Protein
SUBTOTAL				

LUNCH   TIME:

FOOD/BEVERAGE	Calories	Carbs	Fat	Protein
SUBTOTAL				

SNACKS	TIME:			
FOOD/BEVERAGE	Calories	Carbs	Fat	Protein
SUBTOTAL				

DINNER	TIME:			
FOOD/BEVERAGE	Calories	Carbs	Fat	Protein
SUBTOTAL				

TOTAL				

WATER INTAKE

DAILY FOOD GOALS

TARGET	ACTUAL	
		calories
		protein
		carbs
		fat

FITNESS LOG

TO DO

- ☐ ....
- ☐ ....
- ☐ ....
- ☐ ....
- ☐ ....

GOAL FOR TODAY

TIME OF DAY:

CARDIO / OTHER	Heart Rate	Duration	Speed	Level	Intensity	Other	Calories used
SUBTOTAL							

NOTES

TIME OF DAY:

WEIGHTS	Heart Rate	Duration	Speed	Level	Intensity	Other	Calories used
SUBTOTAL							

TOTAL							

VITAMINS / SUPPLEMENTS	DOSAGE	QUANTITY

JOURNAL

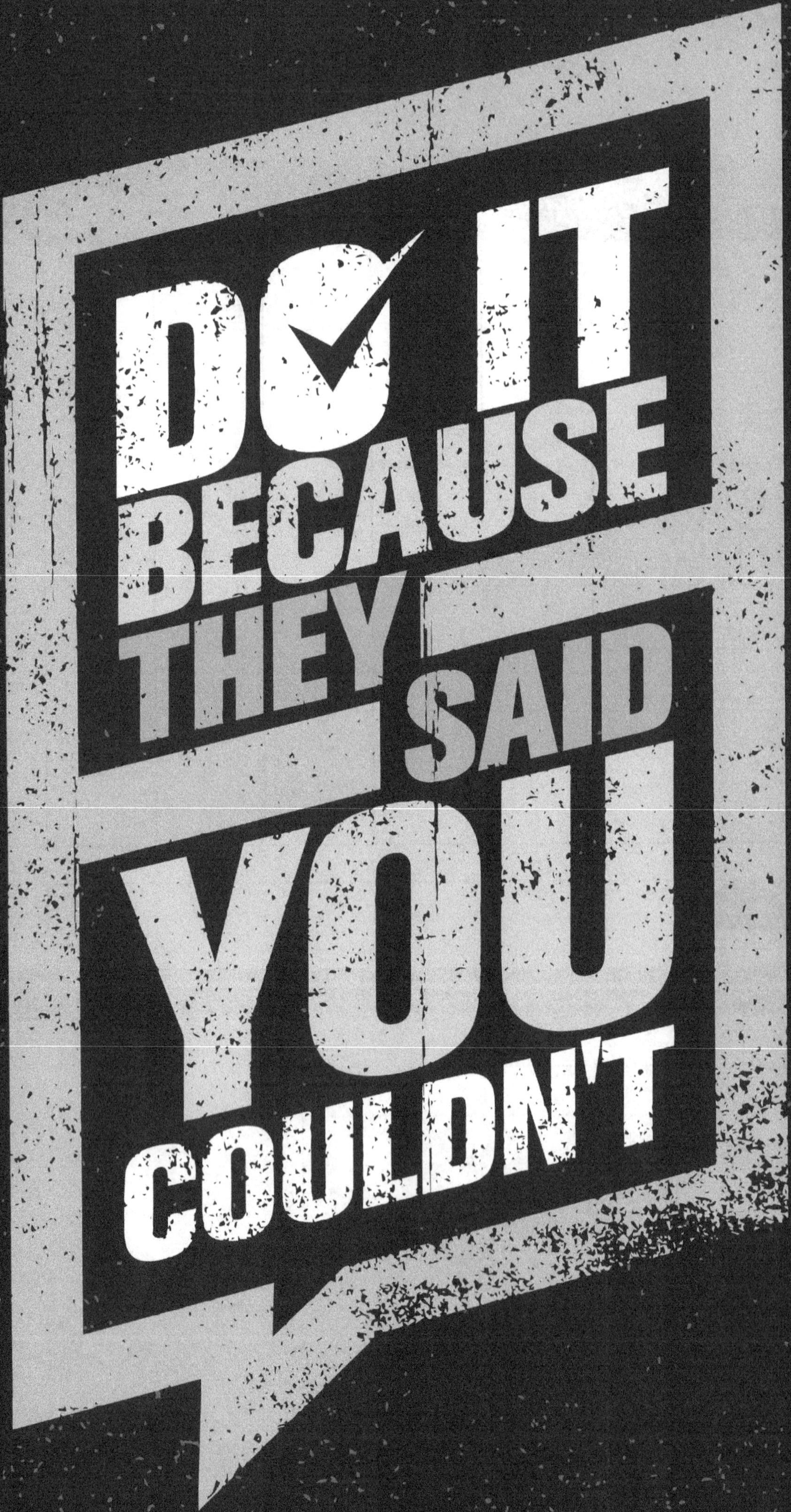
DO IT
BECAUSE
THEY SAID
YOU
COULDN'T

PROGRESS

STATS	Weight	BMI	BMR	Heart Rate	Cholesterol	Blood Sugar	Other

MEASUREMENT

Neck	Shoulder	Chest	Waist

Hip	Thigh	Calf	Arm

NOTES

....

....

....

....

....

....

....

....

....

....

....

....

FOOD LOG

DAY

DATE

WEEK

TO DO

- ☐ ....
- ☐ ....
- ☐ ....
- ☐ ....
- ☐ ....

GOAL FOR TODAY

BREAKFAST		TIME:		
FOOD/BEVERAGE	Calories	Carbs	Fat	Protein
SUBTOTAL				

LUNCH		TIME:		
FOOD/BEVERAGE	Calories	Carbs	Fat	Protein
SUBTOTAL				

SNACKS

TIME:

FOOD/BEVERAGE	Calories	Carbs	Fat	Protein
SUBTOTAL				

DINNER

TIME:

FOOD/BEVERAGE	Calories	Carbs	Fat	Protein
SUBTOTAL				

TOTAL				

WATER INTAKE

DAILY FOOD GOALS

TARGET	ACTUAL	
		calories
		protein
		carbs
		fat

FITNESS LOG

TO DO

- ☐ ....
- ☐ ....
- ☐ ....
- ☐ ....
- ☐ ....

GOAL FOR TODAY

TIME OF DAY:

CARDIO / OTHER	Heart Rate	Duration	Speed	Level	Intensity	Other	Calories used
SUBTOTAL							

NOTES

TIME OF DAY:

WEIGHTS	Heart Rate	Duration	Speed	Level	Intensity	Other	Calories used
SUBTOTAL							

TOTAL							

VITAMINS / SUPPLEMENTS	DOSAGE	QUANTITY

JOURNAL

FOOD LOG

DAY

DATE

WEEK #

TO DO

- ☐ ....
- ☐ ....
- ☐ ....
- ☐ ....
- ☐ ....

GOAL FOR TODAY

BREAKFAST   TIME:

FOOD/BEVERAGE	Calories	Carbs	Fat	Protein
SUBTOTAL				

LUNCH   TIME:

FOOD/BEVERAGE	Calories	Carbs	Fat	Protein
SUBTOTAL				

SNACKS

TIME:

FOOD/BEVERAGE		Calories	Carbs	Fat	Protein
SUBTOTAL					

DINNER

TIME:

FOOD/BEVERAGE		Calories	Carbs	Fat	Protein
SUBTOTAL					

TOTAL					

WATER INTAKE

DAILY FOOD GOALS

TARGET	ACTUAL	
		calories
		protein
		carbs
		fat

FITNESS LOG

TO DO

- ☐ ....
- ☐ ....
- ☐ ....
- ☐ ....
- ☐ ....

GOAL FOR TODAY

TIME OF DAY:

CARDIO / OTHER	Heart Rate	Duration	Speed	Level	Intensity	Other	Calories used
SUBTOTAL							

NOTES

TIME OF DAY:

WEIGHTS	Heart Rate	Duration	Speed	Level	Intensity	Other	Calories used
SUBTOTAL							

TOTAL							

VITAMINS / SUPPLEMENTS	DOSAGE	QUANTITY

JOURNAL

FOOD LOG

DAY	DATE	WEEK #

TO DO

- ☐ ....
- ☐ ....
- ☐ ....
- ☐ ....
- ☐ ....

GOAL FOR TODAY

BREAKFAST		TIME:		
FOOD/BEVERAGE	**Calories**	**Carbs**	**Fat**	**Protein**
SUBTOTAL				

LUNCH		TIME:		
FOOD/BEVERAGE	**Calories**	**Carbs**	**Fat**	**Protein**
SUBTOTAL				

SNACKS — TIME:

FOOD/BEVERAGE	Calories	Carbs	Fat	Protein
SUBTOTAL				

DINNER — TIME:

FOOD/BEVERAGE	Calories	Carbs	Fat	Protein
SUBTOTAL				

TOTAL				

WATER INTAKE

DAILY FOOD GOALS

TARGET	ACTUAL	
		calories
		protein
		carbs
		fat

FITNESS LOG

TO DO

- [ ] ....
- [ ] ....
- [ ] ....
- [ ] ....
- [ ] ....

GOAL FOR TODAY

TIME OF DAY:

CARDIO / OTHER	Heart Rate	Duration	Speed	Level	Intensity	Other	Calories used
SUBTOTAL							

NOTES

TIME OF DAY:

WEIGHTS	Heart Rate	Duration	Speed	Level	Intensity	Other	Calories used
SUBTOTAL							

TOTAL							

VITAMINS / SUPPLEMENTS	DOSAGE	QUANTITY

JOURNAL

FOOD LOG

DAY

DATE

WEEK

TO DO

- [ ] ....
- [ ] ....
- [ ] ....
- [ ] ....
- [ ] ....

GOAL FOR TODAY

BREAKFAST	TIME:			
FOOD/BEVERAGE	**Calories**	**Carbs**	**Fat**	**Protein**
SUBTOTAL				

LUNCH	TIME:			
FOOD/BEVERAGE	**Calories**	**Carbs**	**Fat**	**Protein**
SUBTOTAL				

SNACKS TIME:

FOOD/BEVERAGE	Calories	Carbs	Fat	Protein
SUBTOTAL				

DINNER TIME:

FOOD/BEVERAGE	Calories	Carbs	Fat	Protein
SUBTOTAL				

TOTAL				

WATER INTAKE

DAILY FOOD GOALS

TARGET	ACTUAL	
		calories
		protein
		carbs
		fat

FITNESS LOG

TO DO

- ☐ ....
- ☐ ....
- ☐ ....
- ☐ ....
- ☐ ....

GOAL FOR TODAY

TIME OF DAY:

CARDIO / OTHER	Heart Rate	Duration	Speed	Level	Intensity	Other	Calories used
SUBTOTAL							

NOTES

TIME OF DAY:

WEIGHTS	Heart Rate	Duration	Speed	Level	Intensity	Other	Calories used
SUBTOTAL							

TOTAL							

VITAMINS / SUPPLEMENTS	DOSAGE	QUANTITY

JOURNAL

FOOD LOG

DAY	DATE	WEEK #

TO DO

- ☐ ....
- ☐ ....
- ☐ ....
- ☐ ....
- ☐ ....

GOAL FOR TODAY

BREAKFAST   TIME:

FOOD/BEVERAGE	Calories	Carbs	Fat	Protein
SUBTOTAL				

LUNCH   TIME:

FOOD/BEVERAGE	Calories	Carbs	Fat	Protein
SUBTOTAL				

SNACKS — TIME:

FOOD/BEVERAGE	Calories	Carbs	Fat	Protein
SUBTOTAL				

DINNER — TIME:

FOOD/BEVERAGE	Calories	Carbs	Fat	Protein
SUBTOTAL				

TOTAL				

WATER INTAKE

DAILY FOOD GOALS

TARGET	ACTUAL	
		calories
		protein
		carbs
		fat

FITNESS LOG

TO DO

- ☐ ....
- ☐ ....
- ☐ ....
- ☐ ....
- ☐ ....

GOAL FOR TODAY

TIME OF DAY:

CARDIO / OTHER	Heart Rate	Duration	Speed	Level	Intensity	Other	Calories used
SUBTOTAL							

NOTES

TIME OF DAY:

WEIGHTS	Heart Rate	Duration	Speed	Level	Intensity	Other	Calories used
SUBTOTAL							

TOTAL							

VITAMINS / SUPPLEMENTS	DOSAGE	QUANTITY

JOURNAL

FOOD LOG

DAY	DATE	WEEK #

TO DO

- ☐ ....
- ☐ ....
- ☐ ....
- ☐ ....
- ☐ ....

GOAL FOR TODAY

BREAKFAST

TIME:

FOOD/BEVERAGE	Calories	Carbs	Fat	Protein
SUBTOTAL				

LUNCH

TIME:

FOOD/BEVERAGE	Calories	Carbs	Fat	Protein
SUBTOTAL				

SNACKS

TIME:

FOOD/BEVERAGE	Calories	Carbs	Fat	Protein
SUBTOTAL				

DINNER

TIME:

FOOD/BEVERAGE	Calories	Carbs	Fat	Protein
SUBTOTAL				

TOTAL				

WATER INTAKE

DAILY FOOD GOALS

TARGET	ACTUAL	
		calories
		protein
		carbs
		fat

FITNESS LOG

TO DO

- [ ] ....
- [ ] ....
- [ ] ....
- [ ] ....
- [ ] ....

GOAL FOR TODAY

TIME OF DAY:

CARDIO / OTHER	Heart Rate	Duration	Speed	Level	Intensity	Other	Calories used
SUBTOTAL							

NOTES

TIME OF DAY:

WEIGHTS	Heart Rate	Duration	Speed	Level	Intensity	Other	Calories used
SUBTOTAL							

TOTAL							

VITAMINS / SUPPLEMENTS	DOSAGE	QUANTITY

JOURNAL

PROGRESS

STATS	Weight	BMI	BMR	Heart Rate	Cholesterol	Blood Sugar	Other

MEASUREMENT

Neck	Shoulder	Chest	Waist

Hip	Thigh	Calf	Arm

NOTES

....

....

....

....

....

....

....

....

....

....

....

....

FOOD LOG

DAY

DATE

WEEK #

TO DO

- [ ] ....
- [ ] ....
- [ ] ....
- [ ] ....
- [ ] ....

GOAL FOR TODAY

BREAKFAST   TIME:

FOOD/BEVERAGE	Calories	Carbs	Fat	Protein
SUBTOTAL				

LUNCH   TIME:

FOOD/BEVERAGE	Calories	Carbs	Fat	Protein
SUBTOTAL				

SNACKS

TIME:

FOOD/BEVERAGE	Calories	Carbs	Fat	Protein
SUBTOTAL				

DINNER

TIME:

FOOD/BEVERAGE	Calories	Carbs	Fat	Protein
SUBTOTAL				

TOTAL				

WATER INTAKE

DAILY FOOD GOALS

TARGET	ACTUAL	
		calories
		protein
		carbs
		fat

FITNESS LOG

TO DO

- ☐ ....
- ☐ ....
- ☐ ....
- ☐ ....
- ☐ ....

GOAL FOR TODAY

TIME OF DAY:

CARDIO / OTHER	Heart Rate	Duration	Speed	Level	Intensity	Other	Calories used
SUBTOTAL							

NOTES

TIME OF DAY:

WEIGHTS	Heart Rate	Duration	Speed	Level	Intensity	Other	Calories used
SUBTOTAL							

TOTAL						

VITAMINS / SUPPLEMENTS	DOSAGE	QUANTITY

JOURNAL

FOOD LOG

DAY

DATE

WEEK #

TO DO

- ☐ ....
- ☐ ....
- ☐ ....
- ☐ ....
- ☐ ....

GOAL FOR TODAY

BREAKFAST   TIME:

FOOD/BEVERAGE	Calories	Carbs	Fat	Protein
SUBTOTAL				

LUNCH   TIME:

FOOD/BEVERAGE	Calories	Carbs	Fat	Protein
SUBTOTAL				

SNACKS TIME:

FOOD/BEVERAGE	Calories	Carbs	Fat	Protein
SUBTOTAL				

DINNER TIME:

FOOD/BEVERAGE	Calories	Carbs	Fat	Protein
SUBTOTAL				

TOTAL				

WATER INTAKE

DAILY FOOD GOALS

TARGET	ACTUAL	
		calories
		protein
		carbs
		fat

FITNESS LOG

☐ ....

☐ ....

☐ ....

☐ ....

☐ ....

GOAL FOR TODAY

TIME OF DAY:

CARDIO / OTHER	Heart Rate	Duration	Speed	Level	Intensity	Other	Calories used
SUBTOTAL							

NOTES

WEIGHTS	Heart Rate	Duration	Speed	Level	Intensity	Other	Calories used
SUBTOTAL							

TOTAL							

VITAMINS / SUPPLEMENTS	DOSAGE	QUANTITY

JOURNAL

FOOD LOG

DAY

DATE

WEEK #

TO DO

- ☐ ....
- ☐ ....
- ☐ ....
- ☐ ....
- ☐ ....

GOAL FOR TODAY

BREAKFAST

TIME:

FOOD/BEVERAGE	Calories	Carbs	Fat	Protein
SUBTOTAL				

LUNCH

TIME:

FOOD/BEVERAGE	Calories	Carbs	Fat	Protein
SUBTOTAL				

SNACKS   TIME:

FOOD/BEVERAGE	Calories	Carbs	Fat	Protein
SUBTOTAL				

DINNER   TIME:

FOOD/BEVERAGE	Calories	Carbs	Fat	Protein
SUBTOTAL				

TOTAL				

WATER INTAKE

DAILY FOOD GOALS

TARGET	ACTUAL	
		calories
		protein
		carbs
		fat

FITNESS LOG

TO DO

- ☐ ....
- ☐ ....
- ☐ ....
- ☐ ....
- ☐ ....

GOAL FOR TODAY

TIME OF DAY:

CARDIO / OTHER	Heart Rate	Duration	Speed	Level	Intensity	Other	Calories used
SUBTOTAL							

NOTES

TIME OF DAY:

WEIGHTS	Heart Rate	Duration	Speed	Level	Intensity	Other	Calories used
SUBTOTAL							

TOTAL							

VITAMINS / SUPPLEMENTS	DOSAGE	QUANTITY

JOURNAL

FOOD LOG

DAY

DATE

WEEK #

TO DO

☐ ....

☐ ....

☐ ....

☐ ....

☐ ....

GOAL FOR TODAY

BREAKFAST

TIME:

FOOD/BEVERAGE	Calories	Carbs	Fat	Protein
SUBTOTAL				

LUNCH

TIME:

FOOD/BEVERAGE	Calories	Carbs	Fat	Protein
SUBTOTAL				

SNACKS   TIME:

FOOD/BEVERAGE	Calories	Carbs	Fat	Protein
SUBTOTAL				

DINNER   TIME:

FOOD/BEVERAGE	Calories	Carbs	Fat	Protein
SUBTOTAL				

TOTAL				

WATER INTAKE

DAILY FOOD GOALS

TARGET	ACTUAL	
		calories
		protein
		carbs
		fat

FITNESS LOG

TO DO

- ☐ ....
- ☐ ....
- ☐ ....
- ☐ ....
- ☐ ....

GOAL FOR TODAY

TIME OF DAY:

CARDIO / OTHER	Heart Rate	Duration	Speed	Level	Intensity	Other	Calories used
SUBTOTAL							

NOTES

TIME OF DAY:

WEIGHTS	Heart Rate	Duration	Speed	Level	Intensity	Other	Calories used
SUBTOTAL							

TOTAL							

VITAMINS / SUPPLEMENTS	DOSAGE	QUANTITY

JOURNAL

FOOD LOG

DAY

DATE

WEEK #

TO DO

- ☐ ....
- ☐ ....
- ☐ ....
- ☐ ....
- ☐ ....

GOAL FOR TODAY

BREAKFAST   TIME:

FOOD/BEVERAGE	Calories	Carbs	Fat	Protein
SUBTOTAL				

LUNCH   TIME:

FOOD/BEVERAGE	Calories	Carbs	Fat	Protein
SUBTOTAL				

SNACKS

TIME:

FOOD/BEVERAGE	Calories	Carbs	Fat	Protein
SUBTOTAL				

DINNER

TIME:

FOOD/BEVERAGE	Calories	Carbs	Fat	Protein
SUBTOTAL				

TOTAL				

WATER INTAKE

DAILY FOOD GOALS

TARGET	ACTUAL	
		calories
		protein
		carbs
		fat

FITNESS LOG

TO DO

- ☐ ....
- ☐ ....
- ☐ ....
- ☐ ....
- ☐ ....

GOAL FOR TODAY

TIME OF DAY:

CARDIO / OTHER	Heart Rate	Duration	Speed	Level	Intensity	Other	Calories used
SUBTOTAL							

NOTES

TIME OF DAY:

WEIGHTS	Heart Rate	Duration	Speed	Level	Intensity	Other	Calories used
SUBTOTAL							

TOTAL							

VITAMINS / SUPPLEMENTS	DOSAGE	QUANTITY

JOURNAL

FOOD LOG

DAY	DATE	WEEK #

TO DO

- ☐ ....
- ☐ ....
- ☐ ....
- ☐ ....
- ☐ ....

GOAL FOR TODAY

BREAKFAST   TIME:

FOOD/BEVERAGE	Calories	Carbs	Fat	Protein
SUBTOTAL				

LUNCH   TIME:

FOOD/BEVERAGE	Calories	Carbs	Fat	Protein
SUBTOTAL				

SNACKS — TIME:

FOOD/BEVERAGE	Calories	Carbs	Fat	Protein
SUBTOTAL				

DINNER — TIME:

FOOD/BEVERAGE	Calories	Carbs	Fat	Protein
SUBTOTAL				

TOTAL				

WATER INTAKE

DAILY FOOD GOALS

TARGET	ACTUAL	
		calories
		protein
		carbs
		fat

FITNESS LOG

TO DO

- ☐ ....
- ☐ ....
- ☐ ....
- ☐ ....
- ☐ ....

GOAL FOR TODAY

TIME OF DAY:

CARDIO / OTHER	Heart Rate	Duration	Speed	Level	Intensity	Other	Calories used
SUBTOTAL							

NOTES

TIME OF DAY:

WEIGHTS	Heart Rate	Duration	Speed	Level	Intensity	Other	Calories used
SUBTOTAL							

TOTAL							

VITAMINS / SUPPLEMENTS	DOSAGE	QUANTITY

JOURNAL

DON'T STOP
WHEN IT HURTS
STOP WHEN YOU'RE
DONE

PROGRESS

STATS	Weight	BMI	BMR	Heart Rate	Cholesterol	Blood Sugar	Other

MEASUREMENT

Neck	Shoulder	Chest	Waist

Hip	Thigh	Calf	Arm

NOTES

....

....

....

....

....

....

....

....

....

....

....

....

FOOD LOG

DAY

DATE

WEEK #

TO DO

- ☐ ....
- ☐ ....
- ☐ ....
- ☐ ....
- ☐ ....

GOAL FOR TODAY

BREAKFAST

TIME:

FOOD/BEVERAGE	Calories	Carbs	Fat	Protein
SUBTOTAL				

LUNCH

TIME:

FOOD/BEVERAGE	Calories	Carbs	Fat	Protein
SUBTOTAL				

SNACKS   TIME:

FOOD/BEVERAGE	Calories	Carbs	Fat	Protein
SUBTOTAL				

DINNER   TIME:

FOOD/BEVERAGE	Calories	Carbs	Fat	Protein
SUBTOTAL				

TOTAL				

WATER INTAKE

DAILY FOOD GOALS

TARGET	ACTUAL	
		calories
		protein
		carbs
		fat

FITNESS LOG

TO DO

- ☐ ....
- ☐ ....
- ☐ ....
- ☐ ....
- ☐ ....

GOAL FOR TODAY

TIME OF DAY:

CARDIO / OTHER	Heart Rate	Duration	Speed	Level	Intensity	Other	Calories used
SUBTOTAL							

NOTES

TIME OF DAY:

WEIGHTS	Heart Rate	Duration	Speed	Level	Intensity	Other	Calories used
SUBTOTAL							

TOTAL							

VITAMINS / SUPPLEMENTS	DOSAGE	QUANTITY

JOURNAL

FOOD LOG

DAY	DATE	WEEK #

TO DO

- ☐ ....
- ☐ ....
- ☐ ....
- ☐ ....
- ☐ ....

GOAL FOR TODAY

BREAKFAST   TIME:

FOOD/BEVERAGE	Calories	Carbs	Fat	Protein
SUBTOTAL				

LUNCH   TIME:

FOOD/BEVERAGE	Calories	Carbs	Fat	Protein
SUBTOTAL				

SNACKS

TIME:

FOOD/BEVERAGE	Calories	Carbs	Fat	Protein
SUBTOTAL				

DINNER

TIME:

FOOD/BEVERAGE	Calories	Carbs	Fat	Protein
SUBTOTAL				

TOTAL				

WATER INTAKE

DAILY FOOD GOALS

TARGET	ACTUAL	
		calories
		protein
		carbs
		fat

FITNESS LOG

TO DO

- ☐ ....
- ☐ ....
- ☐ ....
- ☐ ....
- ☐ ....

GOAL FOR TODAY

TIME OF DAY:

CARDIO / OTHER	Heart Rate	Duration	Speed	Level	Intensity	Other	Calories used
SUBTOTAL							

NOTES

TIME OF DAY:

WEIGHTS	Heart Rate	Duration	Speed	Level	Intensity	Other	Calories used
SUBTOTAL							

TOTAL							

VITAMINS / SUPPLEMENTS	DOSAGE	QUANTITY

JOURNAL

FOOD LOG

DAY	DATE	WEEK #

TO DO

- ☐ ....
- ☐ ....
- ☐ ....
- ☐ ....
- ☐ ....

GOAL FOR TODAY

BREAKFAST   TIME:

FOOD/BEVERAGE	Calories	Carbs	Fat	Protein
SUBTOTAL				

LUNCH   TIME:

FOOD/BEVERAGE	Calories	Carbs	Fat	Protein
SUBTOTAL				

SNACKS TIME:

FOOD/BEVERAGE	Calories	Carbs	Fat	Protein
SUBTOTAL				

DINNER TIME:

FOOD/BEVERAGE	Calories	Carbs	Fat	Protein
SUBTOTAL				

TOTAL				

WATER INTAKE

DAILY FOOD GOALS

TARGET	ACTUAL	
		calories
		protein
		carbs
		fat

FITNESS LOG

TO DO

- ☐ ....
- ☐ ....
- ☐ ....
- ☐ ....
- ☐ ....

GOAL FOR TODAY

TIME OF DAY:

CARDIO / OTHER	Heart Rate	Duration	Speed	Level	Intensity	Other	Calories used
SUBTOTAL							

NOTES

TIME OF DAY:

WEIGHTS	Heart Rate	Duration	Speed	Level	Intensity	Other	Calories used
SUBTOTAL							

TOTAL							

VITAMINS / SUPPLEMENTS	DOSAGE	QUANTITY

JOURNAL

FOOD LOG

DAY	DATE	WEEK #

TO DO

- ☐ ....
- ☐ ....
- ☐ ....
- ☐ ....
- ☐ ....

GOAL FOR TODAY

BREAKFAST		TIME:		
FOOD/BEVERAGE	Calories	Carbs	Fat	Protein
SUBTOTAL				

LUNCH		TIME:		
FOOD/BEVERAGE	Calories	Carbs	Fat	Protein
SUBTOTAL				

SNACKS

TIME:

FOOD/BEVERAGE	Calories	Carbs	Fat	Protein
SUBTOTAL				

DINNER

TIME:

FOOD/BEVERAGE	Calories	Carbs	Fat	Protein
SUBTOTAL				

TOTAL				

WATER INTAKE

DAILY FOOD GOALS

TARGET	ACTUAL	
		calories
		protein
		carbs
		fat

FITNESS LOG

TO DO

- ☐ ....
- ☐ ....
- ☐ ....
- ☐ ....
- ☐ ....

GOAL FOR TODAY

TIME OF DAY:

CARDIO / OTHER	Heart Rate	Duration	Speed	Level	Intensity	Other	Calories used
SUBTOTAL							

NOTES

TIME OF DAY:

WEIGHTS	Heart Rate	Duration	Speed	Level	Intensity	Other	Calories used
SUBTOTAL							

TOTAL							

VITAMINS / SUPPLEMENTS	DOSAGE	QUANTITY

JOURNAL

FOOD LOG

DAY

DATE

WEEK #

TO DO

- ☐ ....
- ☐ ....
- ☐ ....
- ☐ ....
- ☐ ....

GOAL FOR TODAY

BREAKFAST

TIME:

FOOD/BEVERAGE	Calories	Carbs	Fat	Protein
SUBTOTAL				

LUNCH

TIME:

FOOD/BEVERAGE	Calories	Carbs	Fat	Protein
SUBTOTAL				

SNACKS

TIME:

FOOD/BEVERAGE	Calories	Carbs	Fat	Protein
SUBTOTAL				

DINNER

TIME:

FOOD/BEVERAGE	Calories	Carbs	Fat	Protein
SUBTOTAL				

TOTAL				

WATER
INTAKE

DAILY FOOD GOALS

TARGET	ACTUAL	
		calories
		protein
		carbs
		fat

FITNESS LOG

TO DO

- [ ] ....
- [ ] ....
- [ ] ....
- [ ] ....
- [ ] ....

GOAL FOR TODAY

TIME OF DAY:

CARDIO / OTHER	Heart Rate	Duration	Speed	Level	Intensity	Other	Calories used
SUBTOTAL							

NOTES

TIME OF DAY:

WEIGHTS	Heart Rate	Duration	Speed	Level	Intensity	Other	Calories used
SUBTOTAL							

TOTAL							

VITAMINS / SUPPLEMENTS	DOSAGE	QUANTITY

JOURNAL

PROGRESS

	Weight	BMI	BMR	Heart Rate	Cholesterol	Blood Sugar	Other
STATS							

MEASUREMENT

Neck	Shoulder	Chest	Waist

Hip	Thigh	Calf	Arm

NOTES

HEALTHY ISN'T A GOAL ITS A WAY OF LIVING

FOOD LOG

DAY	DATE	WEEK #

TO DO

- ☐ ....
- ☐ ....
- ☐ ....
- ☐ ....
- ☐ ....

GOAL FOR TODAY

BREAKFAST   TIME:

FOOD/BEVERAGE	Calories	Carbs	Fat	Protein
SUBTOTAL				

LUNCH   TIME:

FOOD/BEVERAGE	Calories	Carbs	Fat	Protein
SUBTOTAL				

SNACKS TIME:

FOOD/BEVERAGE	Calories	Carbs	Fat	Protein
SUBTOTAL				

DINNER TIME:

FOOD/BEVERAGE	Calories	Carbs	Fat	Protein
SUBTOTAL				

TOTAL				

WATER INTAKE

DAILY FOOD GOALS

TARGET	ACTUAL	
		calories
		protein
		carbs
		fat

FITNESS LOG

TO DO

- [ ] ....
- [ ] ....
- [ ] ....
- [ ] ....
- [ ] ....

GOAL FOR TODAY

TIME OF DAY:

CARDIO / OTHER	Heart Rate	Duration	Speed	Level	Intensity	Other	Calories used
SUBTOTAL							

NOTES

TIME OF DAY:

WEIGHTS	Heart Rate	Duration	Speed	Level	Intensity	Other	Calories used
SUBTOTAL							

TOTAL							

VITAMINS / SUPPLEMENTS	DOSAGE	QUANTITY

JOURNAL

FOOD LOG

DAY

DATE

WEEK #

TO DO

- ☐ ....
- ☐ ....
- ☐ ....
- ☐ ....
- ☐ ....

GOAL FOR TODAY

BREAKFAST   TIME:

FOOD/BEVERAGE	Calories	Carbs	Fat	Protein
SUBTOTAL				

LUNCH   TIME:

FOOD/BEVERAGE	Calories	Carbs	Fat	Protein
SUBTOTAL				

SNACKS   TIME:

FOOD/BEVERAGE	Calories	Carbs	Fat	Protein
SUBTOTAL				

DINNER   TIME:

FOOD/BEVERAGE	Calories	Carbs	Fat	Protein
SUBTOTAL				

TOTAL				

WATER INTAKE

DAILY FOOD GOALS

TARGET	ACTUAL	
		calories
		protein
		carbs
		fat

FITNESS LOG

TO DO

- ☐ ....
- ☐ ....
- ☐ ....
- ☐ ....
- ☐ ....

GOAL FOR TODAY

TIME OF DAY:

CARDIO / OTHER	Heart Rate	Duration	Speed	Level	Intensity	Other	Calories used
SUBTOTAL							

NOTES

TIME OF DAY:

WEIGHTS	Heart Rate	Duration	Speed	Level	Intensity	Other	Calories used
SUBTOTAL							

TOTAL							

VITAMINS / SUPPLEMENTS	DOSAGE	QUANTITY

JOURNAL

FOOD LOG

DAY	DATE	WEEK #

TO DO

- ☐ ....
- ☐ ....
- ☐ ....
- ☐ ....
- ☐ ....

GOAL FOR TODAY

BREAKFAST   TIME:

FOOD/BEVERAGE	Calories	Carbs	Fat	Protein
SUBTOTAL				

LUNCH   TIME:

FOOD/BEVERAGE	Calories	Carbs	Fat	Protein
SUBTOTAL				

SNACKS   TIME:

FOOD/BEVERAGE	Calories	Carbs	Fat	Protein
SUBTOTAL				

DINNER   TIME:

FOOD/BEVERAGE	Calories	Carbs	Fat	Protein
SUBTOTAL				

TOTAL				

WATER INTAKE

DAILY FOOD GOALS

TARGET	ACTUAL	
		calories
		protein
		carbs
		fat

FITNESS LOG

TO DO

- ☐ ....
- ☐ ....
- ☐ ....
- ☐ ....
- ☐ ....

GOAL FOR TODAY

TIME OF DAY:

CARDIO / OTHER	Heart Rate	Duration	Speed	Level	Intensity	Other	Calories used
SUBTOTAL							

NOTES

TIME OF DAY:

WEIGHTS	Heart Rate	Duration	Speed	Level	Intensity	Other	Calories used
SUBTOTAL							

TOTAL							

VITAMINS / SUPPLEMENTS	DOSAGE	QUANTITY

JOURNAL

FOOD LOG

DAY

DATE

WEEK #

TO DO

- ☐ ....
- ☐ ....
- ☐ ....
- ☐ ....
- ☐ ....

GOAL FOR TODAY

BREAKFAST

TIME:

FOOD/BEVERAGE	Calories	Carbs	Fat	Protein
SUBTOTAL				

LUNCH

TIME:

FOOD/BEVERAGE	Calories	Carbs	Fat	Protein
SUBTOTAL				

SNACKS TIME:

FOOD/BEVERAGE	Calories	Carbs	Fat	Protein
SUBTOTAL				

DINNER TIME:

FOOD/BEVERAGE	Calories	Carbs	Fat	Protein
SUBTOTAL				

TOTAL				

WATER
INTAKE

DAILY FOOD GOALS

TARGET	ACTUAL	
		calories
		protein
		carbs
		fat

FITNESS LOG

TO DO

- ☐ ....
- ☐ ....
- ☐ ....
- ☐ ....
- ☐ ....

GOAL FOR TODAY

TIME OF DAY:

CARDIO / OTHER	Heart Rate	Duration	Speed	Level	Intensity	Other	Calories used
SUBTOTAL							

NOTES

TIME OF DAY:

WEIGHTS	Heart Rate	Duration	Speed	Level	Intensity	Other	Calories used
SUBTOTAL							

TOTAL							

VITAMINS / SUPPLEMENTS	DOSAGE	QUANTITY

JOURNAL

FOOD LOG

DAY	DATE	WEEK #

TO DO

- ☐ ....
- ☐ ....
- ☐ ....
- ☐ ....
- ☐ ....

GOAL FOR TODAY

BREAKFAST   TIME:

FOOD/BEVERAGE	Calories	Carbs	Fat	Protein
SUBTOTAL				

LUNCH   TIME:

FOOD/BEVERAGE	Calories	Carbs	Fat	Protein
SUBTOTAL				

SNACKS — TIME:

FOOD/BEVERAGE	Calories	Carbs	Fat	Protein
SUBTOTAL				

DINNER — TIME:

FOOD/BEVERAGE	Calories	Carbs	Fat	Protein
SUBTOTAL				

TOTAL				

WATER INTAKE

DAILY FOOD GOALS

TARGET	ACTUAL	
		calories
		protein
		carbs
		fat

FITNESS LOG

TO DO

- ☐ ....
- ☐ ....
- ☐ ....
- ☐ ....
- ☐ ....

GOAL FOR TODAY

TIME OF DAY:

CARDIO / OTHER	Heart Rate	Duration	Speed	Level	Intensity	Other	Calories used
SUBTOTAL							

NOTES

TIME OF DAY:

WEIGHTS	Heart Rate	Duration	Speed	Level	Intensity	Other	Calories used
SUBTOTAL							

TOTAL							

VITAMINS / SUPPLEMENTS	DOSAGE	QUANTITY

JOURNAL

FOOD LOG

DAY

DATE

WEEK

TO DO

- [ ] ....
- [ ] ....
- [ ] ....
- [ ] ....
- [ ] ....

GOAL FOR TODAY

BREAKFAST		TIME:		
FOOD/BEVERAGE	Calories	Carbs	Fat	Protein
SUBTOTAL				

LUNCH		TIME:		
FOOD/BEVERAGE	Calories	Carbs	Fat	Protein
SUBTOTAL				

SNACKS TIME:

FOOD/BEVERAGE	Calories	Carbs	Fat	Protein
SUBTOTAL				

DINNER TIME:

FOOD/BEVERAGE	Calories	Carbs	Fat	Protein
SUBTOTAL				

TOTAL				

WATER INTAKE

DAILY FOOD GOALS

TARGET	ACTUAL	
		calories
		protein
		carbs
		fat

FITNESS LOG

TO DO

- ☐ ....
- ☐ ....
- ☐ ....
- ☐ ....
- ☐ ....

GOAL FOR TODAY

TIME OF DAY:

CARDIO / OTHER	Heart Rate	Duration	Speed	Level	Intensity	Other	Calories used
SUBTOTAL							

NOTES

TIME OF DAY:

WEIGHTS	Heart Rate	Duration	Speed	Level	Intensity	Other	Calories used
SUBTOTAL							

TOTAL							

VITAMINS / SUPPLEMENTS	DOSAGE	QUANTITY

JOURNAL

PROGRESS

STATS	Weight	BMI	BMR	Heart Rate	Cholesterol	Blood Sugar	Other

MEASUREMENT

Neck	Shoulder	Chest	Waist

Hip	Thigh	Calf	Arm

NOTES

....
....
....
....
....
....
....
....
....
....
....
....

DON'T
FOLLOW
YOUR
DREAMS
CHASE
THEM

CPSIA information can be obtained
at www.ICGtesting.com
Printed in the USA
LVHW060820250323
742590LV00014B/444